📖 READERS

Pre-level 1

Fishy Tales
Colorful Days

Garden Friends
Party Fun

Level 1

A Day at Greenhill Farm
Truck Trouble
Tale of a Tadpole
Surprise Puppy!
Duckling Days
A Day at Seagull Beach
Whatever the Weather
Busy Buzzy Bee
Big Machines
Wild Baby Animals
A Bed for the Winter
Born to be a Butterfly
Dinosaur's Day
Feeding Time
Diving Dolphin

Rockets and Spaceships
My Cat's Secret
First Day at Gymnastics
A Trip to the Zoo
LEGO: Trouble at the Bridge
LEGO: Secret at Dolphin Bay
A Day in the Life of a Builder
A Day in the Life of a Dancer
A Day in the Life of a Firefighter
A Day in the Life of a Teacher
A Day in the Life of a Musician
A Day in the Life of a Doctor
A Day in the Life of a Police Officer
A Day in the Life of a TV Reporter

Level 2

Dinosaur Dinners
Fire Fighter!
Bugs! Bugs! Bugs!
Slinky, Scaly Snakes!
Animal Hospital
The Little Ballerina
Munching, Crunching, Sniffing,
and Snooping
The Secret Life of Trees
Winking, Blinking, Wiggling,
and Waggling
Astronaut: Living in Space
Twisters!
Holiday! Celebration Days
around the World

The Story of Pocahontas
Horse Show
Survivors: The Night the Titanic
Sank
Eruption! The Story of Volcanoes
The Story of Columbus
Journey of a Humpback Whale
Amazing Buildings
LEGO: Castle Under Attack
LEGO: Rocket Rescue
¡Insectos! *en español*
Gigantes de Hierra *en español*
Ice Skating Stars

A Note to Parents

DK READERS is a compelling program for beginning readers, designed in conjunction with leading literacy experts, including Dr. Linda Gambrell, Director of the Eugenge T. Moore School of Education at Clemson University. Dr. Gambrell has served on the Board of Directors of the International Reading Association and as President of the National Reading Conference.

Beautiful illustrations and superb full-color photographs combine with engaging, easy-to-read stories to offer a fresh approach to each subject in the series. Each DK READER is guaranteed to capture a child's interest while developing his or her reading skills, general knowledge, and love of reading.

The five levels of DK READERS are aimed at different reading abilities, enabling you to choose the books that are exactly right for your child:

Pre-level 1 – Learning to read
Level 1   – Beginning to read
Level 2   – Beginning to read alone
Level 3   – Reading alone
Level 4   – Proficient readers

The "normal" age at which a child begins to read can be anywhere from three to eight years old, so these levels are only a general guideline.

No matter which level you select, you can be sure that you are helping your child learn to read, then read to learn!

LONDON, NEW YORK, MUNICH,
MELBOURNE, AND DELHI

Series Editor Deborah Lock
Senior Art Editor Tory Gordon-Harris
U.S. Editor Elizabeth Hester
Design Assistant Sadie Thomas
Production Claire Pearson
DTP Designer Almudena Díaz

Reading Consultant
Linda Gambrell, Ph.D.

First American Edition, 2003
03 04 05 06 07 10 9 8 7 6 5 4 3 2 1
Published in the United States by DK Publishing, Inc.
375 Hudson Street, New York, New York 10014

Published in Great Britain by Dorling Kindersley Limited.

A catalog record for this book is available
from the Library of Congress

ISBN 0-7894-9797-2 (pb) 0-7894-9796-4 (plc)

Color reproduction by Colourscan, Singapore
Printed and bound in China by L Rex Printing Co., Ltd.

The publisher would like to thank the following for
their kind permission to reproduce their photographs:
a=above; c=center; b=below; l=left; r=right t=top;

Ardea London Ltd: 18-19; **Corbis:** Stephen Frink 16-17; Jeffrey L.
Rotman 26-27; **Getty Images:** AEF - Tony Malquist 12t, 28c; Pete
Atkinson 2-3; David Fleetham 20tl; Jeff Hunter 6-7, 30-31; Herwarth
Voigtmann 4-5t; **Nature Picture Library Ltd:** Constantino Petrinos 23tr;
N.H.P.A.: Pete Atkinson 14-15; **Oxford Scientific Films:** Tobias
Bernhard 10-11; **Science Photo Library:** GUSTO 4l.Jacket: **Getty
Images:** Stuart Westmorland front.

All other images © Dorling Kindersley
For further imformation see: www.dkimages.com

Discover more at
www.dk.com

DK READERS

Fishy Tales

DK Publishing, Inc.

Take a
swim in the
blue sea.

snorkel

.lam

Here is a
coral reef.

coral

What do you see?

coral

fish

eye

fin

fish

spot

Small fish
swim in
and out of
the coral.

flipper

 turtles

The turtles play
in the sea.

shell

tail

sea horses

fin

snout

The sea horses
sway to and fro.

13

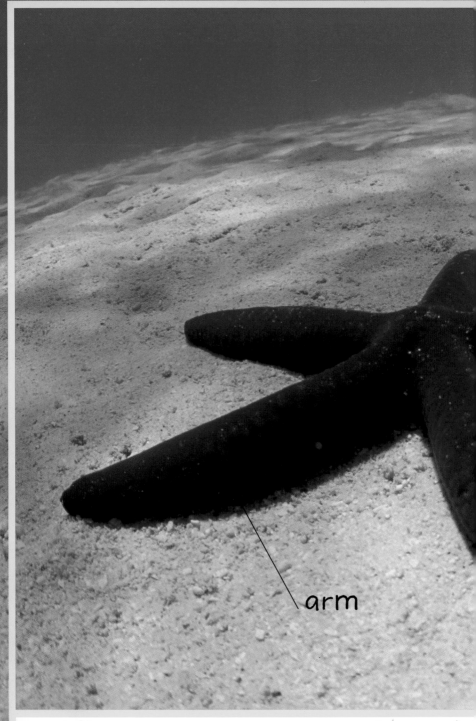

arm

 starfish

Starfish crawl
on the sea floor.

tentacles

jellyfish

Jellyfish
float up
and down
in the sea.

bell

fin

tail

Here comes a shark.
It looks for food.

 sharks

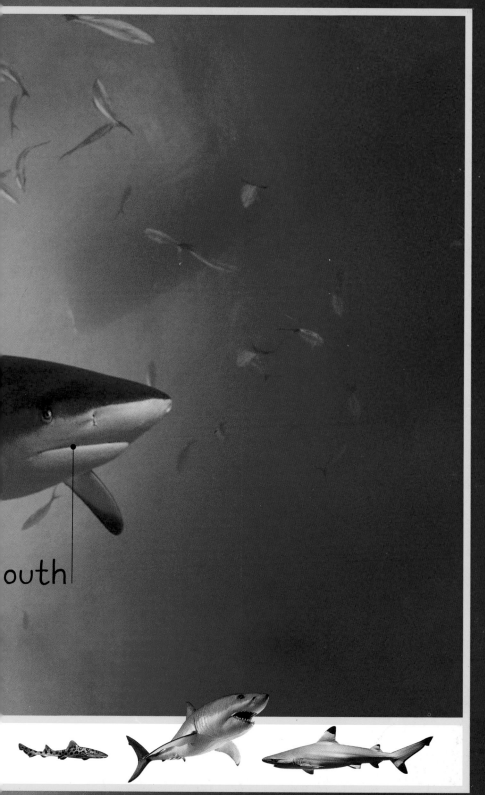

outh

octopuses

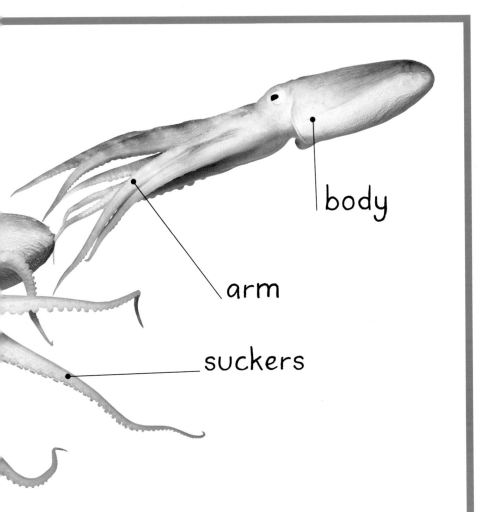

body

arm

suckers

An octopus
shoots off
to hide.

claw

crabs

leg

Crabs hide in
the coral and
in big shells.

shell

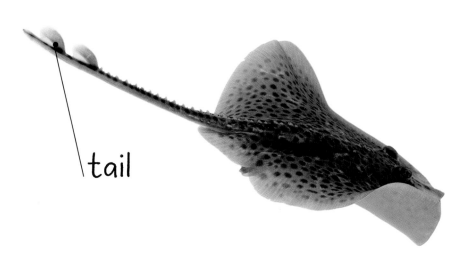

tail

A ray hides on the sea floor.

rays

eye

fin

25

A dolphin swims
away from
the shark.

mouth

dolphins

tail

flipper

Eels look
out for
the shark.

tail

eels

fin

eye

The shark
swims away.

 Can you see ...

fin

gills

nose

a fish ? coral ?

Picture word list

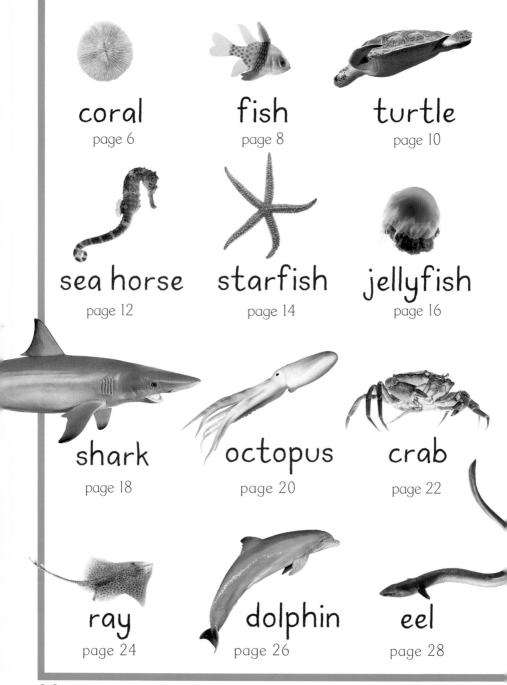

coral
page 6

fish
page 8

turtle
page 10

sea horse
page 12

starfish
page 14

jellyfish
page 16

shark
page 18

octopus
page 20

crab
page 22

ray
page 24

dolphin
page 26

eel
page 28